NO BORDERS

Also by Joseph Bruchac

Fiction:
Arrow Over the Door (1998)
Children of the Longhouse (1996)
Long River (1995)
Dawn Land (1993)

Non Fiction:
Lasting Echoes (1997)
Keepers of Life, co-author Michael Caduto (1994)
Keepers of the Animals, co-author Michael Caduto (1991)
Keepers of the Earth, co-author Michael Caduto (1988)
Survival This Way: Interviews with American Indian Poets (1987)

Storytelling:
Tell Me a Tale (1997)
Roots of Survival: Native American Storytelling and the Sacred (1996)
Native Plant Stores (1995)
Native American Animal Stories (1992)
Thirteen Moons on Turtle's Back, co-author Jonathan London (1992)
Native American Stories from Keepers of the Earth (1991)
Hoop Snakes, Hide-Behinds & Side-Hill Winders, Adirondack Tall Tales (1991)
Return of the Sun: Native American Tales from the Eastern Woodlands (1989)
The Faithful Hunter and Other Abenaki Stories (1988)
Iroquois Stories: Heros and Heroines, Monsters and Magic (1985)
The Wind Eagle: Abenaki Stories (1985)

Poetry:
Translator's Son (1989)
Near the Mountains (1986)
Tracking (1985)

Audio Cassette Tapes:
Keepers of Life (1994)
Keepers of the Animals (1993)
Keepers of the Earth (1991)
The Boy Who Lived With The Bears (1990)
Gluskabe Stories (1990)
Iroquois Stories (1988)

NO BORDERS

NEW POEMS

BY

JOSEPH BRUCHAC

HOLY COW! PRESS • 1999 • DULUTH, MINNESOTA

The author would like to express his deep thanks to the following where
earlier versions of some of these poems were first published:
*A Capella, The Amicus Journal, Bullhead, The Connecticut Review,
Calapooya Collage, Callaloo, Durable Breath,* edited by John Smelcer
(Salmon Run Press), *Earth's Daughters, The Geraldine R. Dodge Foundation
Annual Report, Kestrel, Native American Songs and Poems, an Anthology,*
edited by Brian Swann (Dover Thrift Editions), *Nimrod, Paintbrush,
Phati'tude, Potlatcxh, Salmon Run Pamphlet Series, Sipapu, Today's Poets,
Walt Whitman Birthplace Association, Z Miscellaneous.*

Library of Congress Cataloging-in-Publication Data

Bruchac, Joseph, 1942-
No borders : poems / by Joseph Bruchac.
p. cm.
ISBN 0-903100-84-0 (paperback)
1. Indians of North America—Poetry. 2 Abenaki Indians—Poetry.
I. Title.
PS3552.R794N6 1999
811'.54—dc21   99-10867
CIP

Publisher's Address:

Holy Cow! Press
Post Office Box 3170
Mount Royal Station
Duluth, Minnesota 55803

This project is supported, in part, by a grant from the
Arrowhead Regional Arts Council through an appropriation
from the Minnesota State Legislature, and by generous individuals.

CONTENTS

For all those who see this earth
without maps.

Snowshoeing Across Lake Champlain

At the south end
of Thunder Island
past the lookout point
where a man could watch
for enemy or friend
up lake or down,
cliffs drop a hundred
sudden feet.

Did one of my great-great grandfathers
walk this ice trail to Burlington
where three season's worth of baskets
could be traded for a winter of provisions
or a two-week drunk—
the delicate chance of a family's survival
spun in the brown prism of a rum bottle?

Perhaps it was one
of those ancestors, fire-keepers,
who gave me this answer
when, pushing through the cedars,
not watching my way,
a single branch
like the sinewy arm
of an old man
stopped me
to look down
at the edge falling away
beneath my snowshoes
my heart beating stone sober
and my breath a prayer for balance.

Crossroads Song

Amedzofe, Ghana

Djo ahme, djo ahme, ahme ohhh. . .
give it to me, give me that ancient beat
of drum and heart in syncopated rhythm.

Ko-ko-lio-kwayyyy—
that was the rooster's song,
his claws rattling the rusted tin roof,
wings clopping, the opening eyelids of dawn
rising over red West African hills.

Djo ahme, djo ahme, ahme ohhh

I woke beneath the kente cloth
Chief Ladzekpo placed over me
as I slept like a child, his song and
its patterns a charm against bad dreams,
against my stranger's uncertainties
that had shivered me more
than the hill night's chill.

Djo ahme, djo ahme, ahme ohhh

Opening my eyes, I lifted
my face to the old man's mirror
seeking how my vision
had changed in the shadow
of that thatched hut where I slept.

Djo ahme, djo ahme, ahme ohhh

As I turned to look
through the windowed eye
of the clay house god and saw
his smiling sharktooth mouth
swallow the sacrifice of pale assumptions

I knew then, no matter how many decades,
I would wake and wake and wake again
to the rhythm of that singing sun

Djo ahme, djo ahme, ahme ohhh. . .

The Owl

The Owl, that was the name they called me
as I went without sleep night after night
in that autumn of my twentieth year
as I walked the halls of a college fraternity.
Ko-ko-has Ko-ko-has Ko-ko-has

Sound in the forest of enemy feet
dark faces, the paint dry clay
then the old cry of warning—
Ko-ko-has Ko-ko-has Ko-ko-has
The blood-deep name of spruce smells,
the balsam touch firm underfoot,
soft as wingspread the feathered wind
drawn back, drawn back the ancient song
which is my brother's name.

Ko-ko-has Ko-ko-has Ko-ko-has Ko-ko-has
you waited in trees outside our village
you called to wake us when the pale Long Knives came.
The starlight glittered their metal of thunder
yet we had been drinking their bitter water
and we fell, our blood caught in their dreams.

The wolf Malsum, and Nolka, the deer,
walk beside our waters, my heartbeat stops there
at the wall of skin, the pain of cramped fist
trying to hold that bowstring tight
hearing a name called from sleepless nights
my footsteps echoing down oak halls
among young men who did not speak,
who could not sing the language of birds.

Ko-ko-has Ko-ko-has Ko-ko-has
my own steps fell open, walking forward
into the past forever memory.
I tied one hair to the roots of an ash tree.
They could hold my soul in that place
as surely as they did not hear
that call from a spirit world others still fear
Ko-ko-has, the protector of our dreams.

Walking in Scipio Township

We stopped beside
the oldest willow
rotted at its base,
almost a mouth & lugubrious eyes.

Hearing a whisper, looked up
& saw many leaves
curling toward yellow
after that first touch of cold
the oldest ones here
call Frost Giant's breath.

My friend's son pointed
the waterfall below,
balanced seven summers at an edge
where shale peeled back
milllions of seasons.

And just that morning
I had been reading
Han Shan, the Chinese hermit monk,
who heard such old old voices.

So we listened
to the sound of rocks
& water reflecting
a land made of legends,
waiting further directions
from sun, wind & season

Fallen Ash Tree

The old man
has lain here
so long that his coat
has turned white
with fungus—
a shiver
of tiny filaments.

He is peaceful here
there is no need
to wish for him
to stand again.

Open his old coat,
see the seeds
there waiting
to lift with spring.

Maple Sugaring Moon

Just when the snow begins to leave,
the edges of our northern woods,
the maple trees once more will bring
sweet sap up from their roots.

An Abenaki story said
that maple trees once flowed pure syrup.
All through the year, you only had
to break a twig to fill your birchbark cup.

That was so easy, the people got lazy.
They just stretched out beneath the trees,
mouths open, drinking all through the days.
Glooskap, the giant who helped the people,
saw this was wrong, and so he placed
much water into every maple.

So, to this day, it is not easy
to get our harvest from the trees.
We boil down forty gallons of sap
for every gallon of maple syrup.

But even though Glooskap made it harder,
that work makes our maple syrup taste better.

Leo's Story

Akwesasne Reserve, 1990

There's this thing,
we call it a wolverine,
except it's there out under the water.
Once, when I was little
I was going to dive
when I saw it waiting.
I didn't go in.

Last winter it was out there,
under the ice.
Jimmy Forest's dog
was near an ice hole
when it came right up
and tore its head off.
There was blood there,
red all over the ice.

Yes, we were out
in a boat one time
and we could see bubbles
rising up from the water.
Those bubbles kept moving.
We knew what was there.

It has these two horns
growing out on each side
of its head there on top,
we know what it looks like.
And we know why it's here.
All that booze smuggling,
all that gambling stuff.
We sure know why it's here.

A Bear Song

for N. Scott Momaday

I've learned there are things
our Old People know,
those who remember to keep
their eyes open to an ancient light
seen in dark winter sleep.

Among them is a story I heard
spoken in a sonorous voice,
filled with rumbling
like the throat of a waterfall
when it starts to bring
down the breath of another spring.

It tells of a man who danced.
Few noticed his steps at first.
They seemed awkward and different,
not in step with that rhythm
which moved across the plaza
painted lines of women and men.

But when the drum beat ceased,
that man was no longer there.
All that was to be seen
where his feet met the earth
were the deep prints of a bear.

Desert Tortoise in the Rain

Santa Monica, California

His shell glistens with the moisture
of a early winter rain.
Small drops have drawn him
from his earth-dug bed
beneath porch steps—
all that remains of a house
washed away by fire.

The backyard fence,
which once kept him
from the sight of ocean
or winding canyon,
has also been returned to ash.

The chirr of a wren
can now be heard
from camelia branches
which survived, somehow,
the red flow of flame
to hold new blossoms,
fluttering purple and red
as perfect as Chinese silk.

The tortoise, his head like a lump of lava,
takes one club foot step after another,
bumps his way across heaved red bricks.
He opens his mouth
to let his almost human tongue
loll out to lap up drops
of moisture dark as his eyes.

Then he turns his gaze away
from the sea below to begin his trek
back toward the Mohave
where human hands a decade ago
picked him up to carry him here,
away from his own kind.

As I watch him move
with what some call patience
its seems that words can barely express
what the tortoise knows,
of the rain and the fire
here at the fenced-in edge
of a continent where
our human desires
have come again to nothingness.

Coming Down the Questa Grade
Near San Luis Obispo in a Heavy Rain

That green hill, which shone like Ireland
for just one moment as the sun
came through a slot of cloud before
the breath of mist and spit of sheeted rain
closed in once more, reminded me
of places I've seen and have not seen.

You know what I mean, you've pictured
the vision of Coyote's Hill near Yakima,
the slump of the slope over Yeats' grave.
These are the visioned names of places
here and not here, part of that other way,
like opening your eyes in another's dream.

Wind strips the bark of eucalyptus
like loose wrapping tape trying to bind the rain
and the timeless fronds of Biblical palms
quiver over live oak as the hillside streams
fill their breathless throats to sing,
rattling stones like a shaker of deer bones.

You've heard that music, haven't you?
A rhythm present and then gone again,
to be carried like an obsidian stone
shining in your medicine pouch
filled with things that might have been.

Flying Over Deep Forests

Drops of water slant across the pane,
pushed east by wind, the same wind
which carried the storms that whitened the trees
and now brings the green breath of thaw,
a cycle familiar as freeze, heartbeat, flow.

There are sounds of engines outside the window,
unseen as that wind which pushes winter.
What they seek to shape I cannot tell
but their throats are deep with rhythms of change.

For one moment, I imagine
myself a tree, feeling
as trees feel without this poem,
neither storm nor earthquake
but something set against cycles,
ancient and rooted
as the giant turtle
on whose patient back all earth is placed.

Clear ice of a window
cuts me off from the wind
and at this height
as I grasp my pen
make words on paper
which came from a tree
like those below.
And I know
that I hold no more
than an image
of all that truly shapes or breaks,
goes with or against
the living grain.

Into the Cedar River

I cast my line
into the Cedar River,
watched it pull out of sight
as Adirondack rain began to fall
and thunder walked
over Panther Mountain.

A pulse touched
my fingertips and then
I stripped in line
until a brown trout
lifted from the water
as if seeking to fly
at the end of nylon leader
invisible as hands of wind.

A gust pushed me back
onto mica bright rocks.
I stumbled up the bank,
through rain thicker than breath,
carrying all that the river
consented to give me—

my memory holding the touch
of the trout's smooth fins,
as it left my hands
back into water
as tannin dark
as its vibrant skin.

Coming Down From Hurricane Mountain

John Cheney, the old Adirondack guide
told a story about coming around the corner
up on Hurricane Mountain
when he saw a panther.
It jumped right down in front of him, growling.
"What did you think then?" someone said to him.
"Thought I'd better shoot it," Cheney said.

And this evening, this evening,
coming down that old mountain
I saw two hawks.
One swooped low above my head,
wing feathers spread to hold the sky,
the second was in a spruce tree dead
and dry from the acid in the rain.
Both of them led my sight away
from the gouged earth below
where backhoes and dozers
worked to widen an intersection,
the road flowing
a black dead river.

Then I thought of old
Adirondack John
Cheney's words again.

Geese Flying Over a Prison Sweat Lodge

Fox Lake, Wisconsin

Inside an arch
like that of the sky,
(unlike that arch of mortared stone
with razor wire on top,
which we walk beneath
to find freedom within concrete)
inside the shell of the old turtle,
inside the body of our mother,
inside our memories
waiting to be born again
we hear the sound,
of flock after flock
their ancient calls
of welcome and question,
seeking relatives
after a winter's exile.

Hiss of water on stone,
and the cries of the geese
bark an answer,
their touch deep as bone,
speaking words never written
that always mean home.

Mato

For the Indian Inmates at Fox Lake

There is a place beneath the snow
where the bear has slept.
It remembers its father,
eyes dark as the full night sky.
It remembers its mother,
breath warm as the new spring.

Now, as The Fawn
that wind of the south
returns to the land,
the Old Man's white hair
grows thin and his lodge
made of ice melts again
to a circe of flowers.

Now the bear rises, comes out,
walks its hunger.
Eyes and nose and stomach want
the sweetness of streams,
taste of berries and fish.

It is an old story,
yet I feel it grow new
behind walls and fences
as lengthening days span razor wire
and one Lakota prisoner reaches
as if his fingers could measure the sun.

At Teeheelay Correctional Center for Women

She said
in here
they call me Lauren.
But my real name,
my Winnebago name,
is *Hos-kas-kah,*
Getting in Darkness.

Her words were the first
in a circle of women
on an afternoon
that carried them
away from old names
of judgement and malice
away from all names
without thanks, without grace.

Real names were spoken,
names breathed by grandmothers,
names given to bless themselves.

And as I walked
as I have walked
a thousand times
through prison gates,
I felt the beat
of those names reclaiming
their hearts
the way the throbbing wings
of a thousand geese
took back the sky
as the unbound day moved
into the healing dark.

Worn By the Rain

Holding my father's shotgun in my left hand
I pass it through the sweetgrass smoke,
then touch the shell filled with #6 birdshot
to that wound in my flesh which will not close.

It is dark, clouds hide the starving moon
three days after full, and there is no wind
as I jack the shell into the chamber,
then lift the stock to my shoulder.

I point the barrel to the mourning sky,
towards the southeast and then I say,
Grandfather, I send this back to the place
from which it came. Let the healing start.

The thud of the shot rings in my ears.
The cordite smell is sweet as struck flint,
and somewhere, from its arc of anger,
a green star falls after this thunder.

That night, five winters after his death,
I dream once more my father's voice.
Takwanipihisan, he says. A guide
gave him that word in Newfoundland.

And now it begins, for he speaks
of sky colors, that ancient promise
of peaceful days the Dawn People name
Takwanipihisan—"Coat Worn by the Rain."

Dog Song

Baffin Island, June 1992

I waken to a strange sort of singing,
a high clear voice
so like a child's
that I must go out
into this dawnless dawn
and look in vain
for a human face
as the song continues
ululating and long
without words spoken
in any language.

From the top of that light pole
where he has perched
each early morning
just at this time,
not yet 4 A.M.
old Raven fluffs
his feathers out,
leans forward and
calls down, not at me,
but past me
and far beyond
all these square houses
cars and rutted roads
and dirt caked snowdrifts
which encompass and angle
this town named Apex
wedged at the end
of the road, at the base
of the head-shaped hill.

Raven's call
blurs my eyes
pierces them with a vision
of an older balance,
a bay clean of motors
ice bare of tread marks,
earth bearing no human weights
greater than those of wood, bone, and stone
the humans and animals
still joined together
in that ancient dialogue of survival
and prayer, unbroken by the
high prows of whalers' ships,
the easy thunder
of high-powered rifles.

And Raven's call is
a counterpoint
to the waking song
which rises now
so eerily high
I know it can only
be a sled dog
speaking to sky,
its keening cry
like a mourning child.

Each man's team knows him,
so I learned last night,
each dog knows the
touch of hands and voice,

the familiar balance
of weight on the sled.
There are so few now
on this whole great island
who still run teams
except for Quallunak tourists
on six hour excursions
out from heated hotels,
that I know that dog
wailing in a light wind
was one of those
in Jake Markoosie's team.

They came in with him
a week ago, a long dark line
on the late spring ice
crossing the bay,
coming all the way
from Pangnirtung,
the Caribou place,
a journey a snowmobile
does in hours, a hard trip of days
for a man and his dogs.
That night Jake lurched from town,
stumbled drunk round the house
shouted slurred words in Inuit
which were not curses
and had no translation
saving sorrow and loss.

Two hours ago,
sober Sunday night
Jake looked at me
as we stood by the window
looking over the bay
"It's the best view in town,"
he said and then
"Just a few days ago
I came in from Pang.
I came with my dogs.
I sold my dog team."
Then he turned and walked out
leaving the feel of
that emptiness under
an unsetting Arctic sun.

I heard it first then,
that loneliness echoed
in the long day song
of a mourning dog
at the edge of words
rising, rising,
lost in the long white light.

The Camargue

Southern France, 1991

I.

The land flattens out
like cloth smoothed by a hand
in the delta between
the branching river arms of
le grand and *le petit* Rhone.
We see a reed buzzard,
hawk-wings spread in flight
above a field where
the famous white horses
of the Camargue graze,
heavy-headed, small and stocky,
not easy to break
refusing each generation
to forget the freedom
of living under an open sky,
hooves drumming the sand.

The road bends and then,
behind heavy wire
we glimpse the black bulls
in their wide tideland pastures.
They are slender and agile,
horns shaped like lyres,
found only here in these swamps,
their last refuge from
the humans who hunted them
to extinction on the plains
of all of the rest of Gaul.
Now they live here
only under the sufference
of those who breed them,
not for farming or food

but for the shouts of the ring,
for the *"Corse à la Corcarde,"*
where young men try to pluck
a white cockade
from the horns of a bull.

We do not stop, instead
we roar by at eighty kilometers,
dirt roads winding us
through the Camargue,
above unnamed canals,
along salt-rimed dirt roads edged
by the dark green tangles
of blackberry bushes
heavy with black summer fruit
unpicked and ignored
by our young drivers,
sons of poets
who will not stop
though we reach our arms out,
imagining the sweet taste
of berries like those
our old people honored
with thanksgiving songs.

II.

It was in these ancient tidal lands
that bulls and horses were once truly wild,
not held in by fences on every side.

The horses were white,
prized by their riders
for their toughness and
that sacred color.
The small bulls here
are the blackest of the black,
fierce ones chosen for sacrifice
for two thousand years
within the stone rings
like that in the ancient
Roman amphitheatre at Arles.
"La petite Rome des Gaules,"
it stands in the midst
of T-shirt and postcard vendors,
still used for the bullfights of Provence
still using the brave
black bulls of the Camargue—
grey sand of the thirsty arena
still absorbing the red blood
which shines so brightly
on the black skin of a bull
pierced by the sword,
on the white skin of a horse
gored by a hooking horn.

III.

When we reach the sea at last,
we wind through dunes
where a few flowers,
sand lilies white
as the mane of a Camargue horse,

are in blossom.
We come upon line after line
of camping trailers,
French families clustered together
at the edge of what once was wild
fishing with rods and nets
where the salt flow across the shallow flats
deepens enough for a few fish.

We park the cars
by the sea-edge buildings
and though the sky is wider here
it does not seem
as free to our hearts as the plains
of our own western lands.
Lance goes to look for beer
and Linda walks back
to the dunes to try to find
those white flowers
that we roared past.
Barefooted, I wade across the shallows,
the sand grey and marked by tires.
I pick my way between
the hundreds of small dying coelenterates,
translucent, glistening
beneath the hot sun
like the contents of broken jelly jars.
They float like tiny marker buoys
showing the direction of
the exhausted current.

The five young East Germans
run ahead of me,

take off all of their clothes,
leap into the Mediterranean.
The sand here is pumice fine
and good, someone says in French,
Trés bien for clean skin.
I strip to my shorts,
wade out to my waist.
The water is bathtub warm
more brown than blue
and though I stand quiet
I see little life
only one small green cluster
of sea plants floating
close to the bottom,
two small crabs hiding
in that meagre shelter.

A group of French women
in late middle age
and proper bathing attire
make jokes about the Germans.
People do not bathe naked here.
They are poofs, they say,
clucking their tongues
such nice-looking boys and they are poofs.

But the four young German men
do not hear them
and if they did
they would not care.
They do not see
what I think I see here.
They wrestle like school boys,

leap small waves like horses,
go running wild, angular as storks,
place the seaweed in garlands
on their heads, druids
worshipping an ocean's freedom
which does not reach
their inland city and its wall
which just this year was broken.

IV.

So much human history
makes less of the land.
Memories of the many empires
are written into every European map.
Earth means no more
than territory owned,
baronies and departments,
prefectures and duchys.
Even the sea here is charted
and confined, defined by battles,
equally filled with human sewage
and the wreckage of Rome and Carthage
and more recent armored
dreams of dominion.

And we understand
why our young friends
who brought us to this sacred spot,
revving their engines,

had no thought to stop
to pick the dark fruit
to look close at white flowers
to stand with eyes closed
in the midst of a salt marsh
and feel how it was
when softer feet walked here.

Human invention in such profusion
blinds the perceptions,
closes the eyes
of those who might be native
to see that countenance
which is not human,
the lasting face of the holy earth.
It blocks their ears to
the heartbeat in the sea.
It dulls their touch
so they cannot
feel with every breath
the benediction on their skin
of the open, circling, un-owned wind.

For Pua Kanahele of Hawaii

The mists were thick at the edge
of the caldera, that miles-wide crater
where the red-haired goddess rests
but does not sleep, for on these islands
the fires of creation never cease burning,
and earth is always birthing into ocean.

We stood there together,
faces moist with the tears
of a cool morning rain.
We stood together, but I know
my own feet were tentative at the edge
of that depth which I could not see
while your feet were firm as the roots
of the hau trees which know how to sway
and bend with the strong winds,
like that dance which your people keep
as a prayer and thankgiving, graceful
as wind and bird and flight.

Around us steam rose
from vents in the living skin,
of his great mountain, Mauna Loa,
long mountain, larger
than any other mountain
on the earth.

That warm mist which lifted
was almost the same,
as that which I have tasted often
in the cleansing breath

of the sweat lodge dark
pouring water over lava stones.
You spoke of how you loved to come
as the old people did,
to sit at the edge of these vents
and be washed in Pele's breath.

You had the orange berries in your hand,
you held them close to your heart as you spoke
lifted them as your words became a chant,
and I thank you for those words,
which I could not understand,
though I felt the emotion, felt the song
even as I felt the pain and longing,
the love and sorrow, the loss and the hope
in so many Hawaiian songs, those slack key melodies
that few tourists truly hear.

And although I thank you I know
those words were not for my human ears.
Yet it was a gift
given me to be there
as you cast those berries
in gentle sacrifice to that strength
which no human governments, no bombs
or fences, yet have the power to control.
And I carry the memory of that chant
across the oceans to my own sacred land.

Red Rock

Boulder, Colorado, February 1992

Below Red Rock, a ridge of stone
which juts up, a great animal's spine
above Boulder Creek,
is a place they call Settler's Park.
There a white historical marker
speaks of Niwot, an Arapaho leader
known to whites
as Chief Left Hand.
He asked the gold seekers
who camped in this valley
to go away because he knew
they would cut down the forests,
kill off the game,
leave no food for his children.
He knew their strange hunger
would eat up this land.

As I looked up
I thought of my son's story
of how his Economics teacher
smiled as he lectured,
proving this earth
is only useful for human profit,
laughing at the thought of sacred land.
And of all the students
in that class, eager to please
and earn a good grade,
only my son raised a hand
and argued, unwilling to trade
any part of his heart
for a mark on white paper.

Niwot, you always
spoke for the earth,
always spoke for peace.
An American flag
flew above the camp
your people shared
with Black Kettle's Cheyenne
at Sand Creek that day
when the cowards and bullies
who followed Chivington—
his plan to clear the Indians
from prime land in Colorado—
gave you the wounds
you carried back
to these mountains
which hold your faithful bones.

So I climbed that mountain,
and stood facing the dawn.
My hands on red stones
I prayed in that sunrise,
that all might survive,
even those yet to learn
that though we can destroy
the gifts of this land
we never own them,
only hold them
for the next generation.

On Lenape Land

We stand where land ends
and water begins, green as the back
of Great Turtle's shell where the ancient tree
put out two shoots—first woman, first man.
I place my left hand, the drum-holding hand,
hand close to the heart, on the carved wooden post,
a face facing east, divided black and red,
half in day, half in night.

Cree people, I say, carved such posts as this
for the wabeno, the one chosen by spirits
to heal the unbalanced, see ways into earth,
pierce the hearts of stone with a voice.
Around that mottled pole a serpent circled,
and I think of the story Merwin told
himself the small child
whose innocent hands
held the copperhead snake
crawled into his lap
that slid off then, a slip of light
when his father shouted, leaving the boy
still trusting, hands and heart yet open
to sinewed secrets from earth.

I slowly shape with my hands in air
that snake climbing up the life tree,
then I speak of the hawk carved on its crest
strong gaze seeing further, better than humans,
wings spread to the beat in its chest.

John asks if I feel this village made here,
an imagined reflection of what once was,
is right, if he has listened well
to unearthed stones, faces faced down
to the little people, those guardians of stories
whose eyes look out of knots in gnarled roots,
shapes held in bark and charred woodgrain.

Sometimes, I say, just trust your heart
and if it's right, a sign may come.

As I say this, hand on the pole,
I see the gliding brown and white
of outspread wings as the osprey
swoops from across the lake.
It tries to perch on the branch above,
misses, grasps from below with one foot,
rights to land on the basswood beside us.

Then, as it lifts its feathered crest,
looks back at us with mild fierce eyes
John says, I think I understand.
And we walk quiet, away from there,
placing feet with care on Lenape land.

Inupiaq Whaler on the Browerville Bus

Barrow, Alaska

He shakes his head
as he climbs up the steps.
I'm worn out, he says,
I was up all night
seven hours, cutting up the muktuk.
I'm gonna go home, brush my teeth,
watch an hour of Melrose
and then go to bed.

Fifty-five feet long,
the one we struck
last Sunday and lost.
Found it in the open lead
fifteen miles out from Barrow.
Had to give its spirit a special thanks
for giving itself back to us.
Big whale, that's a lot
of meat to waste.
Stuck up under the ice
it just cooks inside its own skin.
Was it tall?
Hey, I stood up on the fluke
and it was still four feet over my head.
So many guys were climbing on it
I thought we'd wear it out before
we could get all the muktuk.
Hey, take my picture,
I forgot my camera.

He climbs down in Browerville,
loaded down with six shopping bags,
each one labelled MACY'S,
each one filled with black squares of muktuk.

I walk in two worlds with one spirit.

Nothing Vanishes

If nothing physical ever vanishes
without transmutation,
without some trace
without some useful
exchange of atoms,
matter into energy,
time in space
a balanced balance
then in a sense
we all have done
this dance before.

And just as bone
and skin and breath
do not just go to nothingness
so, too, these thoughts
this consciousness
of life in motion
spirit in place
will not simply
just escape
like air from
a broken balloon

or, better yet,
just like that air
will lend some life
to other lungs,
existing changed
and yet if
nothing vanishes
the same
somewhere.

For Louis Littlecoon Oliver

Two Years After His Death

Grandfather Louis,
I am in Oklahoma again
where the Muskogee wind knew your name
and danced a whirling pattern across your path.
Each time you tried to leave, it circled
you back, always back to Indian land.

Though you have departed
there are still elders here
holding the same tough gentleness
that we were given by your last years.
Like the music of a stomp dance song,
the rhythm of your voice has
stretched into our walking breath.

Your old Okie drawl echoes here,
easy to hear as our own heartbeat,
a drum that always helps us remember.

Writing poems, telling jokes, carrying
the sacred fire in your hands,
you walked your gifts
towards us for a time
and then beyond
to another dawn.

When you passed me,
I knelt and scooped a handful
of red earth from your footprint.
It is all I have left of you to touch.
Grandfather, it will have to be enough.

Oligawi

It has been said
in the western world
that sleep is the little brother of death.

But our old people
knew that was not so.

Sleep is older than death,
and dying only
a sort of rest, a path
between dreamings.

Because they knew this
they marked the way,
making shapes on earth
like the old Serpent Mound
to remind us that
our breathing journey
always circles back to earth.

When each new child wakes
for a time they remember
that winding way
they have travelled until
fear and the thickness of speech
comes again between them
and the truth of vision.

We should never forget
that it is not death,
which cradles our nights

with a breath that says
Oligawi, go to sleep unafraid.
Close your eyes and spiral
back into earth's embrace.

What you see with closed eyes
is more real than your waking
and though it can kill you
there never has been
a death to kill sleep,
and there is no darkness
stronger
than dreams,
oligwasi.

*Oligawi: sleep well
*Oligwasi: dream well

Corners

On the corners
in front of package stores
the people lean
into angles of smoke
the wind pushes
to the end of the world

On those sharp corners
they've forgotten a world
once round,
and, forgotten, that wind
blows them over an edge

sharper and more pitiless
than the jagged splinters
of the bottle which falls
and shatters the Thunderbird's wings

An Abenaki Drinking Song

Nidobassis, kagwi padawian?
Ndobiga nothebazi potoya.
Kowanodana

My friend, what have you brought with you?
I went for a bottle and got it.
Kowanodana

Last night I dreamt
I was drinking again
the taste from the brown bottle
was dark and sweet
as a rich confusion of honey
flowing from the comb
while angry bees buzzed about me

Nidobassis, koji milessi?
Nozomi tagastossi ydali
Kowanodana

My friend, will you give me some?
I have none to spare
Kowanodana

I told myself that I
was singing a song
so sweet it would
uproot the roads
and bring back all
our murdered forests
even though my words

were thick on breath
that was slow and shared
by smoke and hard laughter

Nidobassis ngini akwamalsi
Kaguiji nawa kdelalokassi?
Kowanodana

My friend, I am very sick
Well then, what can you do?
Kowanodana

Surrounded by friends
whose faces had no focus,
my hands cold as I gripped
the hard glass
I looked for a reflection
and saw in the mirror
of Wabanaki eyes
a dawn with no sun

Nidobassis n'opchi machinassi
Nidoba sogawiga kadosmi
Kowanodana

My friend, I am dying
Well then, My friend, have a drink
Kowanodana

and when I woke
once again I could see
my grandfather's face
as he stood over me
and said
his voice like the east wind
the one that brings salt
from our old sea
I cannot stand
to see him this way

Kowanodana

In the Place of the Stone

Bare to the waist,
Chief St. Francis
handed me the stone.
See what you can make
out of this—maybe a pipe.

Driving west, we passed
through the wildlife refuge
which a sign named Mississquoi
as though this land did not already
know its own old name,
this land forbidden
by law to Indians
although their traps
never wiped out
the bird and animal people,
although radio voices
measure trees against dollars
selling acid in the rain.

It is a warm day in late autumn
the leaves turning red again
from the gift of the Sky Bear's blood
as I hold in my hand
a shape hidden in stone
and that old voice which speaks to me
says once again:
look through the surface
to find the spirit,
look under the skin
to feel the tough lines of sinew,
the hard, shaping bone.

The Paperbark Tree

written in response to an Australian
Aboriginal story told by Kath Walker

An old woman longed
for her lost tribe.
She searched for their stories
to find them again.

All that she found
were the long cold ashes
from a fire her people
had made long ago.

She sat down by the ashes.
She called the Good Spirit
to help find her people,
help find her their stories.

The Good Spirit heard,
told her what she must do.
Go to those paperbark trees.
Ask for their help.

That was just what she did
and those trees gave her bark.
She took just what was needed,
put that bark in her dillybag.

Then she traveled the earth,
seeking out the dead fires
her tribe kindled before
they want back into Dreamtime.

She picked up the charred sticks
and then drew on the bark,
drew all the lost stories,
the old life of her tribe.

It's that way for us all,
we must find the old fires
before we can draw
out the tales of our tribes.

Then the Dreamtime will find us
in those stories that draw us
in those stories that shape us
and give us back our names.

The Deer Are Calling Us

The deer are calling us
I look into the hills
and I see them in the grey place there
where the line of trees and the stone
of the hillside become one with sky.
We are not a dream, they say.
We have been waiting.

We know you and
the name of your family.

Every year for more than half a century
my father walked into hills like these
to kill the deer with guns that he loved.

I do not know how many times
I helped him
drag their bodies down slopes.
Perhaps it was many times, perhaps
it was only once that I bent
to loop a piece of rope about the horns
and drag the deer back to the camp
pain between my shoulders
as the stiffening body
wore a trail through leaves and snow
before it was hung from the pole in the shed.
Perhaps I am still there, a boy
struggling with the weight
of death at the end of a rope.

My father killed
at least one deer
for every year he walked
this earth
and still the old
understanding remained, never spoken
to men he hunted beside.
The deer he killed were his brothers.

We're ready to die for you
they said and he answered them.

They do not speak
those words to me,
yet wherever I travel
some part of the deer
goes with me
the grey skin case
of my drum, the buckskin shirt,
the moccasins on my feet,
the string
of braided leather around my neck.
As a child, eating
the meat of the deer
I felt them become
a part of me
they made my body,
my sinew and my bones.
I have held the antlers
of slain deer as many times
as I've held the hands of friends.

My sons have never killed a deer,
though they have learned
to walk close enough
to touch a deer, wild in the forest,
and I will not kill a deer again.
Yet the tracks of deer circle our house
and their eyes follow my passage each time
I walk along forest trails as familiar to me
as the streets of a city are to other men.

Each autumn, men
who do not live close to the forest
walk into the hills.
They follow the trails
and the tracks of the deer
and as they follow, deer spirits are around them.
They think they hear the rippling of water
from the streams that flow
but it is the feet of the deer spirits walking.
They think they are touched by wind
but it is the breath of the deer on their faces.
If they put down their guns
and let the fallen leaves embrace them,
let the snow shape itself about them
then a deer woman comes
in the shape of a woman
with eyes more beautiful than any dream
they have ever had before
and leads them, leads them
not over the hills, but into the land.

Sometimes, as one of those men
lays down his gun
and lays down his body
to go with the deer woman
a sudden realization
comes to him, quick
as the silver glint of the rising sun
on ice held by a ledge of stone,
that the search parties
will look for him
in vain and as he looks back
he sees his own bones
and the rags of his clothes
will wait for the crows
in the rain.

To follow the deer
you must fear the deer
without being afraid
of your own death.

The roads which cut through the mountains
the trucks which roar the night
the airplanes which rise up above the earth
as if gravity could not hold them
they are all brief illusions to the spirits of deer
waiting for the engines to end,
waiting for roads to break like dark ice,
for all to fall that must fall.

The deer are calling us,
calling us back into the forest,
back into the hills that remember men
who have forgotten them,
who have forgotten our survival
is a thread of breath,
sad men who have forgotten
those who kill
must know how to pray,
those who kill
must know how to pray.

The Jaguar Farmer

The newspaper pages
carry the stories in black and white
of the Mexican army
entering Yucatan to end
with little violence
a rebellion of Indian peasant farmers.

In Costa Mesa, back from Chiapas,
Edward tells me another story
of rain forest burning and villages
filled with starving Mayan faces.

And once again I hear old Chan K'in
his eyes dark with a century of stories,
telling us the tale as we sat by his fire
of a Lacandon farmer—let us call him K'in Bol,
an ancient name meaning Little Sustainer.

K'in Bol became angry at the forest creatures
because they came and ate food from his milpa.
So he made a prayer and burned incense
before the god-pot of the Lord of Maize.
"You," K'in Bol said, "who protects the farmer,
turn me now into a jaguar, make me quick
and strong so that I can chase away
those useless animals who take my crops."

Akinchob heard that farmer's prayer
and K'in Bol was turned to a jaguar.
His teeth were sharp as the tips of spears,
his claws were swift as the flight of arrows,

his strength was great as a village of men,
his voice grew deep as the rumble of thunder.

But as K'in Bol, the jaguar, guarded his milpa
he saw hungry people gathered around.
He took pity on them and called out loudly,
"My relatives, come in here and eat.
There is plenty of food, I'm just keeping watch
to guard our farm from those useless animals."

So, from that day on, all of the people
of K'in Bol's village stayed far away
from that milpa where the forest creatures
came and went as they pleased
while a great jaguar prowled
and chased away with a voice of thunder
any human who approached that field.

dedicated to Edward James Olmos
and Chan K'in Viejo
March 1995

Spirit Names

Waking up,
looking out a window
in Telluride I see spirit names
written on the sides of buildings.

Manitou Hotel
in block white letters.
Brown siding,
neat green awnings.

All made smaller by the mountain
sloped golden and green
and higher still—
the height of another mountain
unclimbed by feet, uncut by ski slopes—
a half moon hangs
in a cloudless blue sky.

Mountain and moon
spell out names of spirit
which cannot be written—
moving, moving
in and of all.

Waking in the shack
by the mountain road
he hears the sound
of travelers passing.
The road ends here.
The road begins.

The Brown Coat

for my Father, Joseph Bruchac,
who never spoke to me in Slovak

The boy in the old brown fur coat
pulls it close about him.
He has no scarf to keep the wind
from caressing his throat,
from slipping slender fingers of ice
down across the thick muscles of his chest.

His chest tightens
and his body arcs back
as the charged paddles
slam electricity through his skin,
burning through words and paper,
through hair follicles and epidermal tissue,
leaving faint impressions like the pawprints
of a vanished totem.

The coat was his uncle's
worn on the ship, made of the fur
of an animal whose name he does not speak.
It has that animal's musty smell.
When he bends his head, pulling the collar
up around his neck, he hears a song
only part in a human tongue.

He would take off that brown fur coat
if it were not for the wind.
It is a walk of two miles
to the one room school.
There are no trees on these hills,
no trees along this road to break the wind.
All the trees have been cut

to fuel the furnaces, money in the pockets
of the men who own the factories.
There is no money on this road.
Only the wind and the deepening snow.
It is always winter as he walks.

He will walk this way four miles each day,
twenty miles each week, forty weeks each year,
until the years and the weeks and the days
are the length of a road which could have taken
his chilled feet twice around the earth,
but never far enough to reach
a place with the warmth to thaw his breath.

The others laugh at his dark coat,
at the dreaming accent in his voice,
at the one cold baked potato—
all he has in his bag to eat.
There is little sympathy from teachers
who see too many Asian eyes
hear too many impoverished voices
slowed by memories of Eastern Europe.

A story was told about this road,
this road walked in thin third-hand leather,
boots padded with newspaper pages
written in a language my father's children
would never be allowed to read,
that same dialect wrapped about his chest
where paper might break the pity of winter,
a poem in Slovak about bread and the cure for hunger.

There, by the edge of this road, goes the story,
a dark-eyed child removed his coat
stepped out into the wind, a butterfly
released at the wrong season from its chrysalis.
They found him, stiff in new fallen snow,
arms stretched out like an angel embracing a prayer.
When they peeled off the many layers
of ice and thin cloth they found the pages
of newsprint wrapped closest to his body
were now bare of words.
The old language was taken by the wind
or absorbed so deep beneath the skin
no living breath would be strong enough
to bring it forth again.

But that boy did not die just then.
This is the dream he carries with him
as he lifts up from the hospital bed,
as he looks down at the urgent doctor
counting, counting above his body.

He looks down at the face
washed free of care
as the face of a child.
He lets go his breath,
hears a song begin.
It wraps about him
like the coat of an animal
warmed by the language
of the ancient wind.

Singing, he takes
the first steps
toward that mountain,
up the slopes where
all the trees
are tall again.

A Log

There is a log.
Quiet in the woods.
Life on it, within it,
all around it.

But we step over it
on our way elsewhere.

We don't even think
about being that log.

We want to be bright lights.
Stars. In the sky.
Another sun.

Or, at least, an eagle.
Flying. Not at rest.

Instead of that log
we try to pull ourselves
sheer force of will
into the sky.

We need it.
Of course. That log.

In memory of William Stafford

Great Blue Herons

1.

A small boy stands
at the edge of Bear Swamp.
His face is lifted up,
like one wakened from sleep,
his vision caught
by the slow dream motion,
the measured sweep
of the blue heron's flight,
so close one wingtip
touched his shoulder
as if the great bird,
ktsisips, ktsisips, *
had beckoned him
to follow any way he could.

2.

The old people of Mexico,
I have been told,
spoke about the ancient one
a spirit so graceful
in its powerful flight
that in my mind's eye
I, too, could only see it
as Great Blue Heron.

It guarded that land
of swamps and lakes
from which they came,
Aztlan, the Herons' Place.

See how the heron
cocks its head
and pauses
as it goes along?
That is when, they say,
it hears our ancestors' songs

3.

There is a small pool
which is always full
of water flowing in
from Kayaderosseras Creek
sieved through cattails
and arrowroots,
so clear that when
I passed there one dawn
and saw beside it
a doe and two fawns
their images were reflected back
in perfect balance
from the water beside them.

One great blue heron
is often there,
not on the bank,
but waded in,
each step so slow
that its shape
begins and ends
in water, a part
of the endless flow.

4.

The old people say
that there is another
world under our world
there in the water,
everything the opposite
of our own.
When it is summer here,
there it is winter,
on a day in July
just plunge your hand
into that water to feel
December's cold.
And when, in late autumn,
chill touches your heart,
reach in again
and feel the warmth
of a spring held deep
and sure to return.

Blue Heron
is one who has been given
the gift to seek
both land and water
for its life.
One day I see it,
its sword of a beak
spearing fish in the stream
the next day it stalks
the nearby field for mice.
It lives within
both worlds at once.

Here, in this world,
which was made to be
much simpler
and more filled with mystery
than most of our waking
eyes can see
I follow the flight
of the great blue heron
across the canvas
of evening sky
and accept it
as a messenger.

*ktsisips: "great bird" in the Abenaki language

Willows by the Sweat Lodge

My uncle shaped a willow whistle,
breath trembling to call
the Little People.
Peeled wood was pale and clean
as a small child's fingers
smooth with water.

Thrust into soft earth
by the edge of the stream,
our willow wands sprouted deep roots
and now, decades later,
they drift green hair
down to my shoulders.

Their branches are fragile,
yet wherever they touch
moist earth they take root
until each untrimmed willow
is itself a lodge, a circling
house of green branches and leaves.

Some nights, those trees
come into my sleep,
whisper songs
I thought forgotten,
when I wake in the woods,
hearing the feet
of willow people, golden and green,
young deer crossing the shallow stream
in the full moon's light.

Above Jackson Pond

Long-winged, it circled
slow as a heron
yet broader in flight.

Seeking an updraft
to lift it higher,
it flapped wings
darker than clouds,
tail fanned, catching light.

An Eagle.

I whistled its way
and on my third call
it folded wings,
dove and rolled in answer
before flying on
past the tallest pines
which sentinel
the hill above Jackson Pond.

Valleys widen with green,
with the flow of spring,
rivers and lakes
veins pulsing the heart
of the land
held under those wide wings.

Thinking now of that great bird
praising its return,
my own vision opens
to see this earth
more gift than we humans
can give.

Anthology Indians

for Lance Henson

They track us down, I guess
(you said) with the grandsons
of those same scouts
who betrayed Geronimo.
Some of us get clear
of their paper snares
or slip away by changing names
as they try to define us:
one half this, one quarter that.
But sometimes nothing more to prove
that we are who we are
than a memory in blood
which answers no simple definitions.

What *is* it like, they say,
being Indian?
Meaning usual things
like *Do you shave?*
Can you speak the language
and *How come you don't*
wear an Indian suit
like Chief White Eagle
who came and talked
to our school last month?

Hiding behind our tinted glasses,
passing for descendents
of Genghis Khan, somehow
the words come to us again
and the dreams return
telling us the story

of an eagle raised
among the chickens
who no longer wanted
to scratch in the dirt
after seeing the sky.

Louis Oliver and Carroll Arnett
at the Grave of John Ross

Rolling hills are around them,
long blue ridges like those
where the Trail
of Tears began.

A scissortail flycatcher
flies low over the grass,
past the John Ross Pre-School,
the dirt road to the hill
and the grave of the old chief.

Little Coon nods,
quotes words from Bryant.
My old people, he says,
they always taught me
to never walk over a grave.

Gogisgi kneels, wishes
he'd brought his pipe,
places seven day lilies
brought from that edge
where sky flows
blue towards the sunrise.

A black butterfly crosses
their path as they leave
and the old man gestures,
see how those trees
always bow to each other?

Waterfall Near North River

Its flow breaks
from the throat of stone.
Ten thousand seasons
wore through granite
till rock was rippled
to snakesmooth ridges,
sinewed into the Hudson.

Beneath our feet,
the bridge of stone
sounds with a beat
deep as the drums
of Mohawk hunters
who danced thanksgiving
for the gifts of the land
where few hikers now
defy signs posted
to keep earth private.

But in this place
where the depth of water
seen by eyes is never
the same to the step,
the things we leave
are less enduring
than the track of a fawn
in the edge of sand,
the change of current
where a trout
whips the ripple.

The sounds of our passing
will not outlast
either heavy rain
or the rise of water.

The Parrot in Riverside Park

Coming up from the mooring on the Hudson,
where houseboats rock with the turn of tide,
we enter the park on Riverside Drive.

Starting to climb the highest rock,
a stone the color of coal and blood,
we see emerald feathers at the base of an oak.

It is the wing of a winter-killed parrot,
escaped from some open autumn window,
into this brief freedom, two seasons ago.

Trapped with a lime stick, it was shipped
north, far from the jungles we humans destroy
to make pastures or cattle, each fast-food franchise
a styrofoam god, demanding green sacrifice.

Dry sinews barely hold wings to chest,
little is left but bright feathers and bone.
Eyes sunk from sight, its claws are clenched
as if against our December cold.

We place it underneath the stone,
pile leaves and dirt over its wings.
Then we pray for a coming strong wind to sing
its spirit south, a sunrise song
its wings opened towards, remembering.

Spring Peepers

Their voices are thin as lines of rain.
They pierce the night like tribal singers,
threading songs into the beat of the drum,
notes shrill and strong as cries of birth.

I hear them where the edge of the field
slopes down into brush and flowing darkness.
There the swamp fills the night with a presence
more complete than any memory's directions.

Rain falls sudden as seeds from a sower's hands.
It is what they chant for, the high-throated ones.
As they call to each other, they call for moisture,
the rain of new life, where embryo eyes
brighter than jewels surge in masses of eggs.

Finding my way home, I carry their song,
one hand shading my eyes against this cool rain
which soaks through my clothes, beads my brows with crystal,
each drop a note throbbing my skin, singing, singing, singing.

Picking Brussells Sprouts in December

Walking into the garden,
frost breaks under my feet,
like the crumble of ash
from a burned-out fire.

The Brussells sprouts stand
with their thin white coats,
each wide leaf holding a tight green package
like a man coming home from a store
clutching gifts beneath his arms.

The long stem of each plant
where it thrusts up from earth
is like the mottled neck of an okapi,
that rarest of African antelopes,
once thought to only be a myth,
old as the oldest mammals with hooves,
surviving after the others have gone.

It is long after the final harvest
of all the other roots, seeds and shoots.
Except for these plants, the garden is bare.

As I run my hands down
their tough stems, the small heads
break free to thump into the pail.
Their sound is like the beat
of a stick on a drum,
a social dance which circles my feet
into the round house of the seasons,
reminding me at the edge of winter
of the harvests still to come.

Walking

We need to walk
to know sacred places.

Healthy feet feel the heartbeat
of our Mother Earth,
Sitting Bull said long ago.
Walt Whitman knew that, too.

When we go by wheel
we roll over the land
as if it were nothing
but miles left behind.

When we go by air
we cut off our vision
and even our spirits
may take so long
to catch up to our bodies
that our eyes will be empty
of all but flight.

We need to walk
to remember the songs,
not only our own
but those of the birds,
those kept in the arms
of the hills and the wind.

We need to walk
to know sacred places
those around us
and those within.

Seven Moons

AMONG THE VARIOUS NATIVE AMERICAN nations of North America, time was not traditionally reckoned as it is among Europeans. Instead of mechanically counting hours and minutes, American Indian people looked at the position of the sun in the day sky, the moon and stars at night. Instead of dividing the year into twelve months, the Native people talked about thirteen moons. Each moon, a period of about 28 days, had its own name. Those names, which often described what was happening in the natural world at that time of year, varied from one Native American nation to the next just as the ecosystems around them varied. In the northeast, the time of year in early spring when the Maple trees were tapped was called Maple Sugar Moon by the Abenaki. Among the Pomo of California it was Moon of Blooming Flowers. Among the Winnebago of the Great Lakes, it was Fish Running Moon.

In 1992, I co-authored with Jonathan London a children's picture book (illustrated by Thomas Locker) called *Thirteen Moons on Turtle's Back*. But the poems in that book represent only a few of those I've done about the moons. I'm a member of the Abenaki Nation and our own words for those moons are, I think, especially poetic. The following seven poems are part of a year's cycle of poems I've written based on those traditional names and the things the Abenaki people still associate with each of those moons.

KTSI MANIDO
Great Spirit Moon

Anhaldam mawi kassipalilawalan—
Forgive me for whatever wrong
I might have done to you, my friend.
The New Year's greeting
is on all our lips
as we walk beneath
the Great Spirit's Moon.

Wabikokohas, the snowy owl,
has returned from the winter land.
His feathers make patterns
of life and death.
His wings are the shape of stories.

Now as the drifts pile deep,
the oldest tales remember themselves
on the lips of those who share.
The teachings of the animal people,
those who fly and walk,
those who swim and crawl,
are loaned again for us to hear
in stories older than human breath.

In this season when the earth seemed buried
like the bones of our ancestors,
the fire of those ancient histories
reminds us that everything is waiting
unseen, but present, gathering strength
to wake again after this moon of rest.

PIAODOGOS
Boughs Shedding Moon

Moon of winter thaw,
boughs shedding the snow,
as Frost Spirit strides
through the forest
striking his mallet
against the trees.

This hardest of times
is when the stored food
kept in granary baskets
buried under each lodge
would run out in the old days
and hard-eyed starvation
would sit by our fires
while Grandmother Moon
trembled big in the sky,
pity on her old woman's face.

Yet in this moon,
when the hint of spring
can be heard in the sigh
of a warming breeze
and the fall of moist snow
from wet dark branches
with each dawn
the light of the day
is a shadow longer.

MOZOKAS
Moose Hunting Moon

The feet of my brother
break deep furrows
through the frozen snow
in the valleys between ridges
where the buds
at the tips of twigs
are red as blood.

I follow singing,
walking on the weave
of sinew and ash
so that my feet
skim over the crusted snow.

When I am close
as he churns through the drifts,
I loose my arrow into his side.
It bites deep as he runs
and I follow, knowing my brother
will seek a place
where the earth is bare.
Then, as he rolls to dislodge the shaft
the frozen earth drives it in deeper,
cutting at last the cord of his breath.

And this is the moon
when we thank our brother,
when we thank great moose
as we take his hide
to make a robe
to make moccasins.

Yes, this is the moon
when we thank our brother
as we strip his sinew
to make thread for sewing,
as we take his antlers
and bones to make tools
as we share his flesh
with our hungry children.

His gift is so great
that nothing is wasted.

Even his spirit,
accepting our thanks,
remains with us
to strengthen our lives
through this moon
of our brother's sacrifice.

SOGALIKAS
Sugar Moon

The blanket of snow
shrinks back into the soil
as drops of sweet water
form and then fall
from the tips of broken twigs.

Sap fills the bark basket,
rings the new metal bucket,
as the flow begins
linking our present and past.

This gift of the Creator
is an ancient medicine,
from deep within
our Mother's breast
brought by those roots
which reach down
and down
to draw up strength.

So we gather wood,
cleansing the forest,
opening paths summer feet will follow,
stoking many fires
that fill air with steam
as we boil down sap
to the sweetest of tastes.

Long ago,
heated stones
were dropped into buckets
or into the heart of a dugout canoe
filled to the brim with the Maple's gift.

Today, a fire
hisses under
a metal sap pan
as plastic tubes
draw sap into tanks.

But the scent is the same,
the air just as heavy
with clouds of blessing
as it was back then
and this season rejoins us,
trees and human beings,
with generation of thanks.

KIKAS
Planting Moon

The seeds have been held
through another winter,
kept dry and safe
even when our hunger
might have sacrificed
the future.

Like beads of wampum,
they record our belief
in the bargain made
between us and those spirits
of life and growth,
the three sweet sisters—
Corn, Beans and Squash—
who slept while the blanket
of snow covered earth.

Now, where new soil
has been left by the rivers
when they breathed with spring flood,
where weeds turned into ash
in the trembling breath
of fires that opened up the fields,
our deer-horn hoes
caress our Mother's skin.

Then we place the seeds
in mounds shaped with care,
we cover them with songs of faith
in this moon of working prayer.

NOKKAHIGAS
Hoeing Moon

The woman move,
they move together,
move with one rhythm
between the rows.

Green shoots of corn
reach to their ankles,
the beans lift fingers
eager to climb,
the squash begins to
shade the soil
as the women swing hoes
with lazy ease
loosening earth about the roots.

Together, singing,
women and men
pattern the field,
telling stories, laughing.
Work is not labor
when we work together.
The flow of earth
being tilled by the hoe
is the gentle rhythm
of the southern breeze,
the breath of the Fawn
returning at last.

Our songs of hoeing
blend with those of the birds,
whose wings refill
the sky with rainbows.

Rivers sing with us, too,
as the days grow longer,
long as the memory of roots
reaching deep into earth.

This is the moon
that brings back to our eyes
the green blessings of leaves,
the promise of harvest
and harvests to come
warm as the rays
of Elder Brother, the Sun.

MSKIKOIMINAS
Strawberry Moon

The Little People
the guardians of the plants
have done their work well.

Each night as we slept
they went into the fields,
turning the berries
so that every side
could be touched by the dawn.

Now, from the grass,
we see that glow
like embers burning
and the taste of summer
is gathered by our eager fingers.

Old women with baskets
over their arms
sit in the fields,
picking berry after berry,
but tasting none,
saving them to share.

Grandmother Moon
high above the green fields
turns the leaves of berries
into shafts of pure light
as from our lodges
the water drum throb
with our voices
to offer this first harvest
songs of thanks.

Men of the Forest

In the Hanover Zoo
    in Germany,
the orang-utan,
      whose name in Malay
         means "Man of the Forest,"
shambles over
    to the thick plate glass
      answering the signs
        I make with my hands.
Brother
    I see you
      Our Creator
        made both our spirits free

Its eyes
    hold questions
    an elder might ask
      of a child.

So my old people,
    men of the forest,
    were brought to this Europe
      put on exhibit,
      seen as less
        than human.

We hold our hands up
    palm to palm
      feeling the warmth
        of ancestry
          pass
            through the centuries
              and the vanished glass.

About the Author

Joseph Bruchac is an award-winning storyteller, author, and poet. He lives with his wife, Carol, in the Adirondack mountain foothills town of Greenfield Center, New York, in the same house where his maternal grandparents raised him. Much of this storytelling and writing draw on that land and his Abenaki ancestry. Although his American Indian heritage is only part of his ethnic background that includes Slovak and English blood, those Native roots are the ones by which he has been most nourished. With his wife Carol, he is founder and Co-Director of the Greenfield Review Literary Center and The Greenfield Review Press.

His poems, articles and stories have appeared in over 500 publications, from *American Poetry Review* to *National Geographic*. He has authored more than 60 books for adults and children, including *Keepers of the Earth* (with Michael Caduto), *Thirteen Moons on Turtle's Back* (with Jonathan Michael Caduto) and *Turtle Meat and Other Stories* (Holy Cow! Press, 1992).